Plant by Number

Plant by Number

Design Your Dream Garden with 24 Easy, Step-by-Step Planting Plans

Stacy Tornio

Timber Press • Portland, Oregon

Photo and illustration credits appear on page 177.

Timber Press
Workman Publishing
Hachette Book Group, Inc.
1290 Avenue of the Americas
New York, New York 10104
timberpress.com

Timber Press is an imprint of Workman Publishing, a division of Hachette Book Group, Inc. The Timber Press name and logo are registered trademarks of Hachette Book Group, Inc.

Printed in Shenzhen, China (APO), on responsibly sourced paper

Text and cover design by Lauren Michelle Smith
Garden illustrations by Brenda Lyons
The publisher is not responsible for websites (or their content) that are not owned by the publisher.

ISBN 978-1-64326-510-0

A catalog record for this book is available from the Library of Congress.

Contents

Preface

I come from a long line of farmers and gardeners. Growing up, I was surrounded by the beauty of veggies, flowers, and everything in between. Gardening was a big part of my childhood, and it gave me what I believed was a solid foundation for creating my own garden one day.

When I proudly became a homeowner and moved into my first house, I found myself with a nearly blank slate in the front yard—a sunny 20-foot-by-6-foot garden bed, just waiting for my best gardening idea, nearly blank aside from a sweet row of 1970s shrubs established by the previous homeowners. Once those came out, I had a canvas that was all mine, and I was eager to get started.

However, my excitement soon faded, and I even got overwhelmed. I imagined myself strolling through the garden center, selecting whatever caught my eye from the mini-profile pictures on the plant tags. But as I began paying attention to light needs, height, and space requirements, I realized there was more to this than I anticipated. I needed a better approach.

That's when I discovered a game-changer. Bluestone Perennials, an online plant company I found, offered pre-designed garden plans that could be ordered by mail. They had done all the hard work—creating a planting plan, identifying plants that would thrive together, and even providing a layout for the garden.

Admittedly, I was a bit skeptical, but as soon as the plants arrived, I followed the diagram with just a few small modifications and got everything into the ground. The plants were familiar favorites like purple coneflower, black-eyed Susan, liatris, and catmint. Sure enough, within a year or two, my flower bed was thriving and did so for many years. This experience impressed me so much that I started recommending these pre-planned garden beds to anyone who would listen.

It turns out I wasn't alone in my appreciation for pre-designed garden plans. During the ten years I worked at *Birds & Blooms*, a bird and garden magazine, I learned just how popular these plans are among gardeners. We often featured garden plans or container recipes, showing readers exactly how to achieve certain looks. These plans were incredibly popular because they took the guesswork out of gardening. It was just easier.

Even today, when people ask me for plant recommendations, I find myself pointing them to these types of pre-planned garden options. It makes it so easy for anyone, no matter their experience level, to create a beautiful, thriving garden.

This got me thinking—if I love these plans and other gardeners do too, why not create a collection of easy-to-grow, pre-planned gardens that offer even more? Gardens that attract bees, butterflies, birds, and other wildlife, while still being simple and accessible. And so this book was born.

Now I'm excited to share these planting plans with you. Whether you're new to gardening with many spaces to fill, working with a small deck or patio, or just looking to add to an already established garden, there's something here for everyone.

I may not be a great artist when it comes to drawing or painting, but as a kid, I always loved paint-by-number kits because they made art accessible to me. That's what I hope I've done here—made the art of gardening accessible to everyone. I'm giving you the plants and the numbers—now it's up to you to put them into action. Just like my first plant-by-number garden in my twenties, I hope you'll create a garden that brings you beauty and joy for years to come.

Introduction

In 1923, the first patent was filed for the popular paint-by-number technique that many of us know today. By the 1950s, the first paint-by-number kits were created by Max S. Klein, an engineer and owner of the Palmer Paint Sales Company in Detroit, Michigan. Since then, this concept has been replicated in art countless times–and for good reason! Not everyone feels like a natural artist, and these step-by-step methods have empowered people to feel more confident about creating art.

Now it's time to bring that same concept into the gardening world. Instead of painting by number, we're going to be planting by number. The idea is simple: you find the corresponding number on the provided diagram, and you plant the plant assigned said number in that spot. By following the plan closely, you should soon have a thriving, easy-to-care-for garden, whether it's in your front yard, backyard, patio, or deck.

You don't need a green thumb to be successful here. I've selected 50 of the best, easiest-to-grow plants in North America to fit into 24 different plant-by-number plans. These are the plants you see thriving in backyards across the country all season long. After gardening and writing about gardening for more than twenty years, I've seen these plants consistently perform for gardeners time and time again.

While you're welcome to follow the plans exactly, feel free to make modifications as you see fit—more on that in a bit. You can be confident that both the plans and the plants included in them are designed to set you up for success.

This book is laid out in three main sections to guide you through the process:

- **Part 1** provides you with tips for using the planting-by-number method effectively.
- **Part 2** offers 24 step-by-step planting plans, each with a unique theme, to inspire and guide your gardening projects.
- **Part 3** features a Plant Directory that corresponds to the numbers in the diagrams, allowing you to learn more about each plant, including detailed profiles and tips for growing them successfully.

So sit back, relax, and explore the different planting plans. See what inspires you. This planting-by-numbers method is a fantastic way to create the garden of your dreams.

The Basics of Plant by Number

Gardening can be a fulfilling and rewarding activity, but for many, the idea of planning and planting a garden from scratch can be overwhelming. That's where the idea of "planting by numbers" comes in to help. Much like the classic paint-by-number kits that guided budding artists, this approach to gardening takes the guesswork out of creating a beautiful, thriving garden.

By following pre-designed plans with numbered diagrams, you can confidently plant your garden with the assurance that you're setting yourself up for success. In this section, we'll explore the basics, from understanding the plants featured to making your own modifications and ensuring your garden meets the specific needs of each plant.

Learn about the Plants Featured

There are 50 total plants featured in this book, carefully selected for their ease of growth and versatility. These plants are not only resilient but are also capable of thriving in most parts of North America. The idea behind this selection was to ensure that you can "plant it and forget it" for the most part, with minimal maintenance required beyond regular watering.

As someone who has gardened since childhood and written about gardening for over twenty years, I've seen that certain plants consistently appear in gardens and on the "best of" plant lists. And there's a good reason for this—they work. You'll often see these same plants thriving in public gardens and backyards across the country because they're reliable and beautiful.

In this book, you'll find a mix of trees and shrubs, perennials, and annuals that are not only resilient but also great for creating stunning garden spaces. For each plant in the planting plan, you can refer to the Plant Directory in part 3 of the book to explore its profile, ensuring it's a good fit for your space.

Understand the Benchwarmers

The "benchwarmers" are alternative plants that can be swapped into the planting plans as needed. For example, if a plan calls for purple coneflowers but you prefer the look of classic white Shasta daisies or golden tones of black-eyed Susans, feel free to make the swap. While the benchwarmers aren't listed as direct replacements for specific plants within each plan, they do offer you the freedom to customize your garden according to your preferences.

In some cases, if a planting plan includes an ornamental grass, you might find a different grass listed as a benchwarmer. However, you're not limited to swapping grass for grass—you might decide to include two grasses or substitute something entirely different. The goal is for you to feel empowered to make these plans your own, tailoring them to fit your personal style and gardening needs.

Explore Other Varieties and Cultivars

Within any plant family, there are often numerous varieties and cultivars to choose from. For instance, the black-eyed Susan family includes more than two dozen native species. This diversity means that when buying plants, it's important to look for the botanical name to ensure you're getting the right plant. However, don't be afraid to explore other options, especially if you're looking for specific colors, sizes, or characteristics.

Cultivars offer unique traits that can enhance your garden in different ways. For example, there's a black-eyed Susan cultivar called 'Goldsturm' known for its long bloom time, and another called 'Cherry Brandy' that boasts striking pink blooms instead of the traditional yellow. As you gain more experience with gardening, you'll

enjoy researching and experimenting with different varieties and cultivars, particularly if you have specific needs like limited space or a desire for a particular color scheme.

Make Your Own Layout Modifications

The garden plans provided can be followed exactly as they are, with clear instructions on which plants to buy and where to place them. However, these plans are also flexible, allowing you to adjust the overall size or shape of the garden to fit your space. If you have a smaller area, simply reduce the number of plants. If you have a larger space, feel free to add more plants to fill it out.

While it's important to keep the size and space needs of each plant in mind, don't hesitate to modify the layout to suit your garden's unique dimensions. The key is to make the garden work for you, ensuring that the final result is both functional and beautiful.

Discover Light Needs for Different Plants

Light is a crucial factor for plant growth, and it's important not to overlook the light needs of the plants in your garden. Each plant's general light requirements are listed in the Plant Directory, but it's always a good idea to check the plant tags when purchasing, whether from a local garden center or online. While the profiles provided in this book are comprehensive, new varieties or cultivars may have slightly different light preferences.

It's also essential to assess the light conditions in your garden realistically. You might think of an area as sunny, but if you take a closer look, it could be shaded for much of the day. Make sure you know the actual light levels in each area of your garden before selecting plants, as this will help you place them in spots where they'll thrive.

Know Soil and Water Requirements

For many of the plants featured, you'll notice moist, well-draining soil is preferred. This is a common requirement, but not everyone has perfect soil conditions. If you're trying to grow a plant with specific soil needs, it's important to assess whether your garden's soil can meet those

requirements. For example, if your soil is sandy and drains too quickly, you might need to amend it or choose plants that are more tolerant of such conditions.

Water requirements are another critical consideration. While all plants need water, some are more demanding than others. It's important to be realistic about whether you can meet a plant's moisture needs, especially if it requires frequent watering. Many of the plants listed are drought-tolerant, but this doesn't mean they never need water—especially when they're first being established. Newly planted plants typically need more water to get off to a strong start, so be mindful of their needs during this crucial period.

Understand Size and Space Needs

One of the most common mistakes gardeners make is underestimating how large plants will grow. It's easy to overlook this when you're excited about

getting your plants in the ground, but it's important to check the plant label for both height and width at maturity. This information can be hard to gauge from a diagram, but it's crucial for ensuring that your plants have enough space to thrive.

If a plant is expected to grow 6 feet tall and 4 feet wide, you'll need to space them accordingly to avoid overcrowding. While it's fine for plants to grow near each other and create a lush garden, you don't want them competing for space, which can lead to poor growth and health issues.

Start Choosing Your Plants

Plant by Number is designed to make gardening approachable, enjoyable, and successful for everyone, regardless of experience level. By understanding the plants featured, making thoughtful modifications, and paying attention to light, soil, and space needs, you can create a thriving garden that reflects your personal style and the unique conditions of your space.

Whether you're following the plans exactly or making them your own, the key is to embrace the process and enjoy the journey of watching your garden grow.

Plant-by-Number Garden Plans

Gardening for Birds, Bees, and Butterflies

I want a bee garden.

Transform your garden into a haven for bees with this planting plan. Featuring a variety of blooms, this plan will attract and support a wide range of pollinators. Perfect for all levels of gardeners, these plants will enhance the beauty and biodiversity of your outdoor space.

Bee Balm

This aromatic flower is a favorite among bees, providing abundant nectar and adding a splash of color to your garden.

Hydrangea

With its large, showy blooms, hydrangea attracts bees and other pollinators, creating a stunning focal point in your garden.

Phlox

Phlox flowers come in a variety of colors and attract bees with their sweet fragrance and plentiful nectar.

Veronica

Also known as speedwell, veronica plants produce spiky flowers that bees love, adding texture and visual interest to your garden.

Native Plant Tip

Many species of bee balm genus *Monarda* are native to North America, providing essential nectar for bees. If you're looking for another native option, consider planting wild bergamot (*Monarda fistulosa*).

Garden Tip

Plant a variety of flowers that bloom at different times throughout the growing season to provide ongoing nectar for bees. Avoid using pesticides, as they can harm pollinators.

These numbers correspond to the plant profiles in the Plant Directory, which begins on page 117.

Plants:

- Bee balm (3)
- Hydrangea (28)
- Phlox (38)
- Veronica (48)

Benchwarmers:

Buttonbush (10)
Catmint (12)
Liatris (31)

I want a garden for butterflies.

You'll see fluttering all around your yard with this butterfly-friendly planting plan! By incorporating these four plants, you'll attract a variety of beautiful butterflies to your garden. This plan is perfect for anyone who wants to support local wildlife and enjoy a colorful, dynamic outdoor space.

Butterfly Weed

These vibrant orange flowers are a magnet for butterflies, providing nectar and serving as a host plant for caterpillars.

Floss Flower

With its fluffy blue blooms, floss flower attracts butterflies and adds a charming touch to your garden.

Lamb's Ear

Lamb's ear offers soft, silvery foliage that provides a resting spot for butterflies, making it a delightful addition to any garden.

Spirea

This versatile shrub produces clusters of small flowers that attract butterflies, adding both beauty and structure to your garden.

Native Plant Tip

Butterfly weed (*Asclepias tuberosa*) is a native plant that provides essential nectar for butterflies and serves as a host plant for their larvae. For another native option, try planting swamp milkweed (*Asclepias incarnata*).

Garden Tip

Incorporate a variety of nectar-rich plants that bloom at different times to provide a continuous food source for butterflies throughout the growing season. Avoid using pesticides, as they can harm these delicate pollinators.

Plants:

- Butterfly weed (9)
- Floss flower (21)
- Lamb's ear (30)
- Spirea (45)

Benchwarmers:

Bee balm (3)

Milkweed (33)

Penstemon (36)

I want a garden for hummingbirds.

Transform your garden into a haven for hummingbirds with this planting plan! By incorporating these five plants, you'll attract these tiny fliers and also enjoy a colorful landscape. This plan is ideal for gardeners of all experience levels who want to support local wildlife.

Buttonbush

This native shrub produces clusters of fragrant, nectar-rich flowers that are a magnet for hummingbirds and other pollinators.

Cardinal Flower

With its striking red blooms, cardinal flower is a favorite of hummingbirds, providing ample nectar throughout the summer.

Penstemon

Penstemon, also known as beardtongue, features tubular flowers that are perfect for hummingbirds, offering both nectar and beauty for your garden.

Rose of Sharon

This hardy shrub produces abundant flowers that attract hummingbirds, adding a splash of color and interest to this plan.

Salvia

Salvia plants, with their vibrant spikes of bloom, are a reliable nectar source for hummingbirds, bringing both color and fragrance to your garden.

Native Plant Tip

Buttonbush is relatively low-maintenance and can adapt to various soil types, but it performs best in rich, organic soil. Mulching around the base can help retain moisture and provide nutrients.

Garden Tip

Plant flowers in clusters rather than single plants. Hummingbirds are more likely to visit a group of flowers, as it offers a more abundant and attractive source of nectar.

Plants:

- Buttonbush (10)
- Cardinal flower (11)
- Penstemon (36)
- Rose of Sharon (40)
- Salvia (42)

Benchwarmers:

Coral bells (14)
Lungwort (32)
Spirea (45)

I want to feed the birds.

Create a bird-friendly oasis with this simple planting plan! By incorporating these five plants, including both annuals and perennials, you'll attract a variety of seed-eating birds. Whether you're an experienced gardener or just beginning, this plan will help you support local wildlife and add beauty to your outdoor space.

Black-Eyed Susan

This bright, cheerful flower is a magnet for birds and pollinators, providing seeds and nectar throughout the summer.

Cosmos

With its delicate, feathery foliage and vibrant blooms, cosmos attracts birds and beneficial insects, adding a touch of whimsy to your garden.

Feather Reed Grass

This elegant grass offers seeds and shelter for birds while adding vertical interest and movement to your landscape.

Purple Coneflower

Known for its striking, long-lasting blooms, purple coneflower is a favorite among birds for its plentiful seeds.

Sunflower

Towering sunflowers provide abundant seeds for birds, making them a must-have in any bird-friendly garden.

Native Plant Tip

Many purple coneflowers are native—it depends on the variety—but if you're looking for other alternatives, try pale purple coneflower (*Echinacea pallida*).

Garden Tip

With seed-bearing plants like these, don't clean out your garden in fall—keep those plants up so the seeds will dry and feed the birds.

Plants:

- Black-eyed Susan (5)
- Cosmos (16)
- Feather reed grass (20)
- Purple coneflower (39)
- Sunflower (47)

Benchwarmers:

Coreopsis (15)
Fountain grass (22)
Joe Pye weed (29)

I want to create a bird habitat.

Transform your garden into a thriving bird habitat with this curated planting plan! By incorporating these four plants, you'll create a space that provides food, shelter, and nesting sites for a variety of birds. This plan is perfect for gardeners who want the sights and sounds of birds in their outdoor space.

Beautyberry

With its bright purple berries, beautyberry provides an important food source for birds in fall and winter while adding striking color to your garden.

Dogwood

Dogwood trees and shrubs offer berries, shelter, and nesting sites for birds, making them a versatile addition to a bird-friendly garden.

Elderberry

Elderberry bushes produce clusters of berries that attract birds, and their dense foliage provides excellent cover and nesting opportunities.

Fountain Grass

This ornamental grass adds texture and movement to your garden while providing seeds and shelter for birds.

Native Plant Tip

Flowering dogwood (*Cornus florida*) is a native tree that offers bright red berries in fall, providing a critical food source for birds. Its branches also offer excellent nesting sites and cover.

Garden Tip

Offer birds a variety of plants that are sources of food and shelter throughout the year. Incorporate berry-producing shrubs and trees, seed-bearing grasses, and dense foliage to create a diverse and inviting habitat.

Plants:

- Beautyberry (2)
- Dogwood (18)
- Elderberry (19)
- Fountain grass (22)

Benchwarmers:

Feather reed grass (20)
Ninebark (34)
Viburnum (49)

Low-Maintenance Gardening

I want a perennial flower garden.

Transform your garden into a perennial paradise with this curated planting plan! By incorporating these five plants, you'll enjoy vibrant blooms year after year. This plan is perfect for gardeners who want a low-maintenance, colorful garden.

Aster

Asters are late-blooming perennials that produce clusters of daisy-like flowers in shades of purple, blue, and white. They attract butterflies and other pollinators, making them a vital addition to any garden.

Black-Eyed Susan

Black-eyed Susan is a hardy perennial that produces bright yellow flowers with dark centers. It is excellent for attracting bees and butterflies and provides a long blooming season from summer to fall.

Daylily

Daylily is a versatile perennial known for its trumpet-shaped flowers that come in a variety of colors. It's easy to grow and maintain, with each flower typically lasting just one day, though the plant produces many blooms.

Goldenrod

Goldenrod is a tall, yellow-flowering perennial that blooms in late summer and fall. It attracts a variety of pollinators and is often mistakenly blamed for hay fever, which is actually caused by ragweed.

Purple Coneflower

Purple coneflower, also known by its botanical name, *Echinacea*, is a popular perennial with large, purple-pink daisy-like flowers. It is drought-tolerant, attracts pollinators, and is known for its medicinal properties.

Native Plant Tip

Aster is a native plant that provides late-season nectar for pollinators and birds. Its abundant flowers bloom in late summer and fall, offering essential resources when other plants have finished blooming.

Garden Tip

Incorporate native species to promote local wildlife and reduce maintenance. Regular deadheading and dividing of perennials will keep your garden vibrant and healthy.

1 5 1 5 1 5

39 17 26 39 17 26 39 17 26

Plants:

- Aster (1)
- Black-eyed Susan (5)
- Daylily (17)
- Goldenrod (26)
- Purple coneflower (39)

Benchwarmers:

Milkweed (33)

Russian sage (41)

Shasta daisy (44)

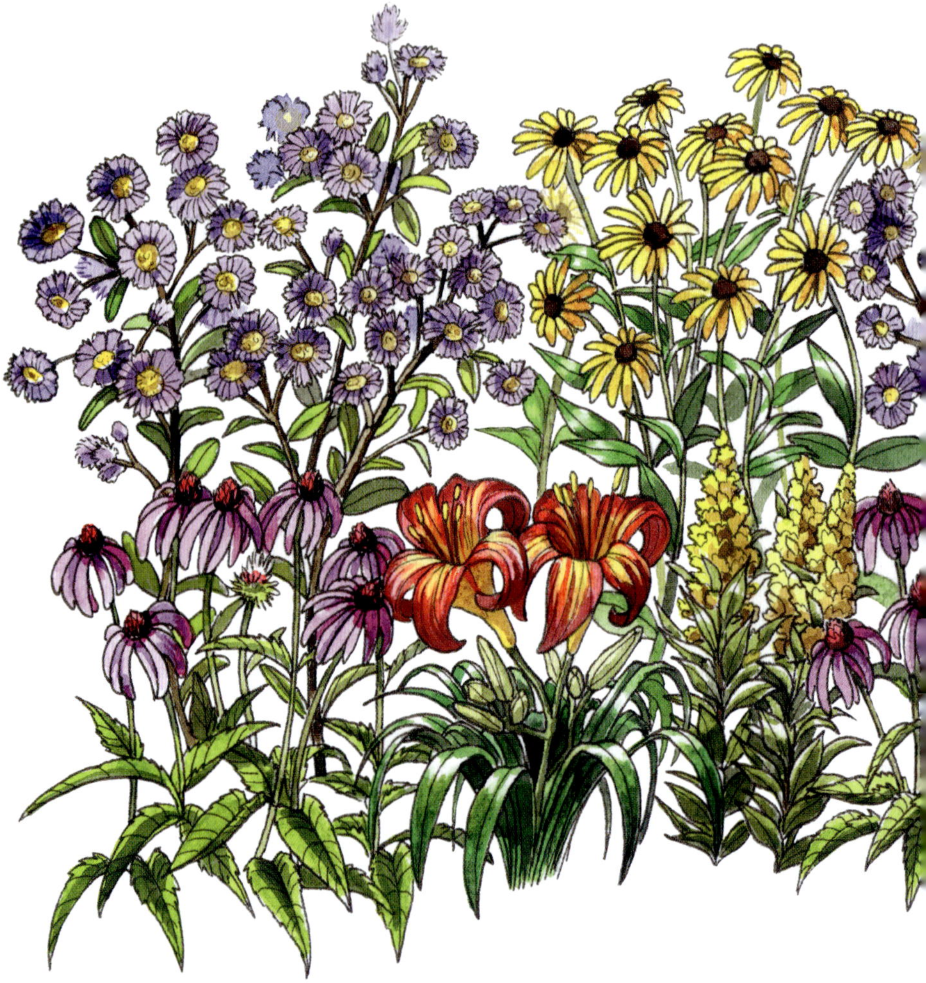

I want a garden filled with shrubs.

Transform your garden into a lush, shrub-filled oasis with this curated planting plan. By incorporating these four shrubs, you'll enjoy year-round beauty and support local wildlife. This plan is perfect for gardeners looking to add structure and variety to their outdoor space.

Beautyberry

Beautyberry bushes are prized for their vibrant purple berries that persist into winter, providing both visual interest and food for wildlife. Their arching branches and small, pinkish flowers in the summer add to their appeal.

Elderberry

Elderberry produces clusters of small, dark berries that are highly attractive to birds and other wildlife. In addition to their ecological benefits, elderberries can be used to make syrups, jams, and wines.

Hydrangea

Hydrangea is a popular ornamental shrub known for its large, showy flower heads, which can range in color from white to pink, blue, and purple.

Viburnum

Viburnum shrubs offer year-round interest with their fragrant spring flowers, colorful berries, and attractive foliage. They are hardy, versatile plants that provide excellent habitat and food for birds and pollinators.

Native Plant Tip

Arrowwood viburnum (*Viburnum dentatum*) is a native shrub known for its adaptability and resilience. It produces clusters of white flowers in late spring, followed by blue-black berries that attract birds.

Garden Tip

Prune shrubs selectively to maintain shape and encourage healthy growth. Regularly mulch and water your shrubs to keep them thriving.

Plants:

- Beautyberry (2)
- Elderberry (19)
- Hydrangea (28)
- Viburnum (49)

Benchwarmers:

Buttonbush (10)
Dogwood (18)
Ninebark (34)

I want to grow a garden from seed.

Create a stunning garden by growing from seed with this curated planting plan. By incorporating these three easy-to-grow plants, you'll enjoy vibrant blooms and attract pollinators all season long. This plan is perfect for gardeners who want the satisfaction of starting plants from seed.

Cosmos

Cosmos is a fast-growing annual that produces delicate, daisy-like flowers in a range of colors. It's perfect for filling in gaps and adding a light, airy touch to your garden.

Sunflower

Sunflower is an iconic garden plant known for its tall stalks and large, sunny blooms. It is easy to grow from seed and provides food for birds and pollinators.

Zinnia

Zinnias are vibrant, long-blooming annuals that thrive in sunny spots. They come in a variety of colors and shapes, making them perfect for adding bold splashes of color to your garden.

Native Plant Tip

Maximilian sunflower (*Helianthus maximiliani*) is a native North American sunflower that thrives in a variety of soil types and produces bright yellow blooms in late summer to fall. It's excellent for attracting pollinators and provides seeds for birds, making it a valuable addition to your garden.

Garden Tip

Start your seeds indoors or directly in the garden after the last frost date. Ensure they have plenty of sunlight and water regularly to promote healthy growth. Thin seedlings as needed to prevent overcrowding and encourage strong, vigorous plants.

Plants:

- Cosmos (16)
- Sunflower (47)
- Zinnia (50)

Benchwarmers:

Columbine (13)
Four o'clocks (23)
Milkweed (33)

I want an easy garden with natives.

You'll have a low-maintenance haven with these easy-to-grow native plants. By incorporating these four plants, you'll support local wildlife and enjoy beautiful blooms with minimal effort. This plan is perfect for gardeners seeking simplicity and sustainability.

Columbine

Columbine is a delicate perennial with unique spurred flowers that attract hummingbirds and bees. It's perfect for shady spots and adds an elegant touch to your garden.

Coreopsis

Coreopsis, also known as tickseed, is a hardy perennial with bright yellow flowers that bloom profusely. It's drought-tolerant and attracts butterflies, making it a cheerful addition to your garden.

Milkweed

Milkweed is essential for monarch butterflies, providing both nectar and a place to lay eggs. It's a resilient plant that thrives in various conditions and supports a diverse range of pollinators.

Purple Coneflower

Purple coneflower, or echinacea, is a popular native perennial with large, daisy-like flowers. It's drought-resistant and attracts bees, butterflies, and birds, adding both beauty and ecological value to your garden.

Native Plant Tip

Swamp Milkweed (*Asclepias incarnata*) is a native plant ideal for moist areas in your garden. It produces clusters of fragrant pink flowers that attract monarch butterflies and other pollinators. Its deep roots help stabilize soil and improve water retention.

Garden Tip

Choose native plants that are well-adapted to your local climate and soil conditions to ensure success with minimal maintenance. Group plants with similar water and sunlight needs together to create a cohesive, thriving garden. Mulch regularly to retain moisture and suppress weeds, and enjoy the natural beauty and benefits of your native plant garden.

Plants:

- Columbine (13)
- Coreopsis (15)
- Milkweed (33)
- Purple coneflower (39)

Benchwarmers:

Blanket flower (6)
Goldenrod (26)
Liatris (31)

I want a garden with long-lasting blooms.

Enjoy a garden that provides continuous color with long-lasting blooms by incorporating these hardy plants. This selection ensures vibrant flowers throughout the growing season, adding long-term beauty to your outdoor space.

Aster

Asters are perennials that bloom in late summer to fall, offering clusters of star-shaped flowers. They attract butterflies and provide a burst of color when many other plants have finished blooming.

Black-Eyed Susan

Black-eyed Susans are resilient perennials with bright yellow petals and dark centers. They bloom from summer to early fall and are excellent for attracting bees and butterflies.

Catmint

Catmint is a hardy perennial known for its long blooming period from late spring to fall. Its lavender-blue flowers and aromatic foliage make it a lovely addition to any garden.

Coreopsis

Coreopsis, or tickseed, is a perennial that produces bright yellow flowers from early summer to fall. It's drought-tolerant and attracts a variety of pollinators.

Purple Coneflower

Purple coneflowers are long-blooming perennials with large, daisy-like flowers. They bloom from summer to fall and attract bees, butterflies, and birds, adding both beauty and ecological value to your garden.

Native Plant Tip

Yellow coneflower (*Echinacea paradoxa*) is a unique native coneflower that produces striking yellow blooms from midsummer to early fall. It is drought-tolerant and attracts bees, butterflies, and other pollinators, making it a valuable addition to a garden with extended blooming periods.

Garden Tip

To ensure long-lasting blooms, deadhead spent flowers regularly to encourage new growth. Provide adequate water and nutrients, and mulch to retain moisture and suppress weeds, creating a thriving and vibrant garden.

Plants:

- Aster (1)
- Black-eyed Susan (5)
- Catmint (12)
- Coreopsis (15)
- Purple coneflower (39)

Benchwarmers:

Geranium (25)
Petunia (37)
Veronica (48)

Gardening by Color

I want a purple garden.

Transform your garden into a serene purple paradise with this selection of plants. By incorporating these blooms, you'll enjoy a striking garden filled with shades of purple throughout the growing season.

Bluebells

Bluebells produce clusters of bell-shaped, purple-blue flowers in spring. They thrive in shady areas and create a carpet of color that signals the start of the growing season.

Catmint

Catmint is a hardy perennial known for its aromatic foliage and spikes of lavender-blue flowers. It blooms from late spring to fall, providing continuous color and attracting pollinators.

Liatris

Liatris, also known as blazing star, features tall, feathery spikes of purple flowers. It blooms in late summer and adds vertical interest to the garden while supporting pollinators.

Native Plant Tip

Mountain bluebells (*Mertensia ciliata*) is a native perennial that produces clusters of vibrant blue flowers late spring to early summer. It thrives in moist, well-drained soils and is perfect for adding a splash of color to your purple garden.

Garden Tip

To maintain a cohesive purple theme, regularly deadhead flowers to encourage new blooms and keep the garden looking fresh.

Plants:

- Bluebells (8)
- Catmint (12)
- Liatris (31)

Benchwarmers:

Bellflower (4)

Floss flower (21)

Veronica (48)

I want a yellow garden.

Sunny days are ahead when you brighten your garden with a vibrant yellow theme. This selection of plants is sure to make a statement, with cheerful blooms that provide continuous color and flower. In turn, this means you'll attract and support pollinators throughout the growing season.

Black-Eyed Susan

Black-eyed Susans are hardy perennials with bright yellow petals and dark centers. They bloom from summer to early fall and attract bees and butterflies.

Coreopsis

Coreopsis, also known as tickseed, is a perennial that produces abundant bright flowers. It's drought-tolerant and perfect for adding yellow to any garden.

Sunflower

Sunflowers are iconic garden plants known for their tall stalks and large, cheerful blooms. They are easy to grow from seed and provide food for birds and pollinators.

Native Plant Tip

Coreopsis is always an excellent native perennial that produces bright yellow flowers from late spring to early summer. It's naturally drought-tolerant and easy to grow, making it a great choice for adding long-lasting color to your yellow-themed garden.

Garden Tip

Add a layer of organic mulch to help retain soil moisture, suppress weeds, and provide nutrients, keeping your garden healthy and low maintenance.

Plants:

- Black-eyed Susan (5)
- Coreopsis (15)
- Sunflower (47)

Benchwarmers:

Daylily (17)

Goldenrod (26)

Zinnia (50)

I want a pink garden.

Transform your garden into a pink paradise with this selection of plants. These vibrant blooms will add a touch of elegance and attract pollinators throughout the growing season. Perfect for gardeners looking to create a serene and visually appealing space, this plan incorporates a variety of pink flowers that will provide continuous color and support for local wildlife.

Aster

Asters are perennials that produce clusters of star-shaped, pink-purple flowers in late summer and fall. They attract butterflies and add late-season color to your garden.

Phlox

Various cultivars of phlox feature dense clusters of small, fragrant flowers, and many come in pink. Look for mildew-resistant varieties. All attract butterflies, making them an excellent choice for your garden.

Purple Coneflower

Despite its name, purple coneflower is a hardy perennial with large, pinkish-purple flowers. It blooms from summer to fall and attracts bees, butterflies, and birds.

Rose of Sharon

Rose of Sharon produces large, hibiscus-like flowers—look for cultivars in shades of pink. It blooms from midsummer to fall and adds a tropical feel to your garden.

Native Plant Tip

A cultivar of phlox, *Phlox paniculata* 'Jeana', is a native perennial known for its clusters of fragrant pink flowers that bloom from midsummer to fall. This variety is particularly attractive to butterflies and resistant to mildew.

Garden Tip

Ensure your garden receives adequate sunlight and regular watering, particularly during dry spells. Adding organic matter to soil will improve fertility and drainage, helping your plants flourish.

Plants:

- Aster (1)
- Phlox (38)
- Purple coneflower (39)
- Rose of Sharon (40)

Benchwarmers:

Bleeding heart (7)
Fuchsia (24)
Hydrangea (28)

I want a red garden.

Red flowers are always a good choice in the garden because they stand out. Focusing on a variety of red blooms will definitely add to the garden's drama. Best of all, these flowers naturally attract area wildlife—especially hummingbirds, which are known for their attraction to red.

Bee Balm

Bee balm is a vibrant perennial with bright red, tubular flowers that bloom in mid to late summer. It attracts bees, butterflies, and hummingbirds, adding both color and activity to your garden.

Cardinal flower

Look for spikes of flowers that bloom from midsummer to early fall. Cardinal flower thrives in moist soil and partial shade, making it perfect for adding a splash of red to wetter areas of your garden.

Coral Bells

Coral bells are known for their attractive foliage and delicate red (or pink) flower spikes that bloom in late spring to early summer. They are versatile perennials that thrive in both sun and partial shade.

Native Plant Tip

It's not exactly red blooms, but another native to check out is eastern bee balm (*Monarda bradburiana*). It's a native perennial known for its pale pink to lavender flowers, often with reddish-purple spots.

Garden Tip

For all color gardens, planting in clusters will increase the impact. You can also enhance the vibrancy by mixing in plants with dark green or silver foliage as a contrasting backdrop.

Plants:

- Bee balm (3)
- Cardinal flower (11)
- Coral bells (14)

Benchwarmers:

Geranium (25)

Penstemon (36)

Salvia (42)

I want a white garden.

This selection of elegant plants will add a touch of sophistication while supporting pollinators throughout the growing season. Ideal for gardeners who want to create a tranquil and visually appealing space, this plan delivers.

Hydrangea

'Annabelle' hydrangea is a cultivar of smooth hydrangea (*Hydrangea arborescens*) known for its large, round clusters of pure white flowers that bloom from early summer to fall. This variety can thrive in a range of soil conditions.

Shasta Daisy

Love classic white, daisy-like flowers with yellow centers? Shasta daisy blooms from early summer to fall, giving you that elegant look all season.

Summersweet

Summersweet produces fragrant white flower spikes in mid- to late summer, thriving in moist, well-drained soils and attracting a variety of pollinators.

Native Plant Tip

Here's another hydrangea to know about. Oakleaf hydrangea (*Hydrangea quercifolia*) is a native shrub known for its large, cone-shaped clusters of white flowers that gradually turn pink as they age. Its distinctive, lobed leaves resemble oak leaves and provide stunning red and purple fall foliage.

Garden Tip

With hydrangea, prune in late winter or early spring to encourage new growth and more abundant blooms. Adding mulch around the base will help retain moisture and keep roots cool.

Plants:

- Hydrangea (28)
- Shasta daisy (44)
- Summersweet (46)

Benchwarmers:

Ninebark (34)

Viburnum (49)

Gardening for Containers

I want a container for hummingbirds.

Elevate your outdoor space with a vibrant container garden designed to attract hummingbirds. These selected plants will provide nectar-rich blooms that hummingbirds love, adding lively movement and color to your patio, deck, or balcony.

Petunia

These flowers thrive in containers with well-drained soil and full sun, providing continuous blooms throughout the season.

Salvia

This one is a hummingbird favorite, particularly types with bright red flowers. You can find annual and perennial options, and while you often see the annual in containers, both can work well.

Zinnia

Zinnias are cheerful annuals that offer vibrant, nectar-rich blooms in a range of colors, including shades of red and pink that attract hummingbirds. They are easy to grow in containers, needing full sun and regular watering.

Native Plant Tip

There are lots of salvia to choose from, and here's another. Scarlet sage (*Salvia coccinea*) is a native plant known for its bright red flowers that bloom throughout the summer and fall. It's particularly attractive to hummingbirds and thrives in containers with well-drained soil and full sun.

Garden Tip

If you want to double or triple the chances of seeing hummingbirds in your garden, then add an extra container or even a sugar-water feeder. More options can definitely make a difference.

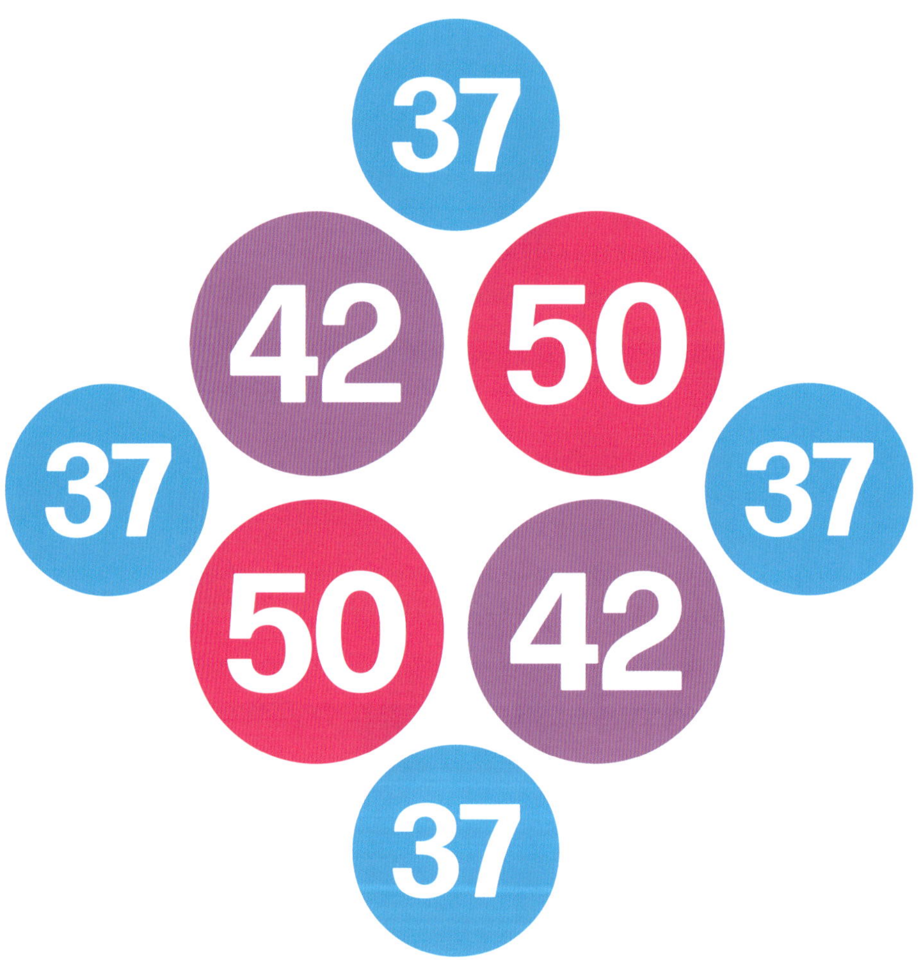

Plants:

- Petunia (37)
- Salvia (42)
- Zinnia (50)

Benchwarmers:

Columbine (13)
Four o'clocks (23)
Fuchsia (24)

I want a container with lots of blooms.

Brighten your patio or balcony with a container garden filled with an abundance of blooms. These selected plants will provide vibrant, long-lasting flowers, ensuring a colorful display throughout the growing season.

Geranium

Geraniums are popular annuals that produce clusters of bright, colorful flowers. They thrive in containers, needing well-drained soil and full sun to partial shade, and bloom continuously from spring through fall.

Petunia

Petunias are versatile annuals with nonstop flowers available in a wide range of colors. They perform exceptionally well in containers, requiring well-drained soil and full sun for optimal blooming.

Salvia

Both annual and perennial salvias will truly give you blooms for the entire container season. Check with your local garden center to see which varieties they have.

Native Plant Tip

Salvia can come in multiple colors. *Salvia farinacea* is a native perennial known for its spikes of blue to violet flowers that bloom from late spring to frost. It does well in containers with sun and well-drained soil.

Garden Tip

For a container garden with abundant blooms, choose a large container to provide enough space for root growth and a high-quality potting mix that retains moisture while providing good drainage.

Plants:

- Geranium (25)
- Petunia (37)
- Salvia (42)

Benchwarmers:

Four o'clocks (23)
Pansy (35)
Zinnia (50)

I want a container for butterflies.

Invite butterflies to your patio or balcony with a container garden designed to attract these beautiful pollinators. The selected plants will provide nectar-rich blooms that butterflies love, ensuring a lively and colorful display throughout the growing season.

Bellflower

These bell-shaped flowers come in shades of blue and purple. They thrive in containers with well-drained soil and full sun to partial shade, providing continuous blooms that attract butterflies.

Floss Flower

These fluffy, blue to purple blooms are particularly attractive to butterflies. They do well in containers, needing full sun and regular watering to keep the soil evenly moist.

Pansy

Pansies are cool-season annuals with bright, cheerful flowers in a variety of colors. They are perfect for containers, requiring well-drained soil and partial to full sun.

Native Plant Tip

Connect with local butterfly organizations that are knowledgeable about native plants in your area. These groups can provide valuable advice and recommendations tailored to your specific region.

Garden Tip

Regularly deadhead spent flowers to encourage continuous blooming, and avoid using pesticides, which can harm butterflies. Place your container in a sunny spot and consider adding a shallow dish with water and a few stones for butterflies to rest on while they drink.

Plants:

- Bellflower (4)
- Floss flower (21)
- Pansy (35)

Benchwarmers:

Catmint (12)
Phlox (38)
Zinnia (50)

Other Garden Solutions

I want a shade garden.

Shady areas shouldn't be ignored. Turn your shaded spots into lush, colorful spaces with this selection of shade-loving plants. These plants will thrive in low-light conditions, adding texture and color to your garden.

Bleeding Heart

Bleeding hearts are known for their delicate, heart-shaped pink or white flowers that hang from arching stems. They thrive in partial to full shade and moist, well-drained soil, adding a whimsical touch to your garden.

Bluebells

The bell-shaped blue flowers of these plants emerge in early spring. They prefer shady, moist conditions and provide a burst of color to shaded garden areas.

Coral Bells

Gardeners love coral bells for their vibrant foliage and delicate flower spikes. They do well in partial shade and well-drained soil, adding texture and color with their variety of leaf colors.

Hosta

Hostas are shade-loving perennials with large, attractive leaves and tall flower spikes. They thrive in full to partial shade and are perfect for adding lush greenery to shaded areas of your garden.

Lungwort

These plants have clusters of pink, blue, or white flowers and speckled foliage that adds interest to the shade garden. Lungwort thrives in partial to full shade and moist, well-drained soil.

Native Plant Tip

Virginia bluebells, a native plant, is perfect for adding early-season color to your shade garden and highly attractive to pollinators like bees and butterflies.

Garden Tip

Don't be disappointed if your plants don't take off right away. When establishing a new garden, especially in heavy shade, it might take some time to get going.

Plants:

- Bleeding heart (7)
- Bluebells (8)
- Coral bells (14)
- Hosta (27)
- Lungwort (32)

Benchwarmers:

Columbine (13)
Pansy (35)
Summersweet (46)

I want a big garden.

If you have a big space to fill, this is the garden plan for you. This selection of easy-to-grow plants will add a mix of textures, colors, and heights, creating a dynamic and visually appealing garden. Adjust it to fit your specific needs, adding more or fewer plants to make it work for your space.

Aster

Asters are hardy perennials that produce clusters of star-shaped flowers in late summer and fall. They add vibrant color to your garden and attract pollinators, thriving in full sun to partial shade and well-drained soil.

Butterfly Weed

This is a low-maintenance perennial that is also a host plant for monarchs. It's a standout in any large garden, and you can feel good knowing you're supporting the butterfly population.

Coreopsis

Coreopsis, also known as tickseed, is a versatile perennial with bright yellow flowers that bloom from early summer to fall. It is drought-tolerant and thrives in full sun, adding a cheerful splash of color to your garden.

Daylily

Daylilies are hardy perennials known for their trumpet-shaped flowers that come in a variety of colors. They bloom from early summer to fall and thrive in full sun to partial shade, making them ideal for large garden spaces.

Dogwood

Dogwood trees and shrubs offer beautiful spring blooms, attractive foliage, and bright red berries in fall. They thrive in full sun to partial shade and well-drained soil, adding structure and year-round interest to your garden.

Ninebark

Ninebark is a hardy shrub known for its attractive, peeling bark and clusters of white or pink flowers. It thrives in full sun to partial shade and well-drained soil, providing texture and interest to your garden throughout the year.

Phlox

This plant has clusters of fragrant flowers in a variety of colors from midsummer to early fall. It thrives in full sun and well-drained soil, attracting butterflies and adding vibrant color to your garden.

Native Plant Tip

Butterfly weed is a native perennial known for its bright orange flowers that bloom from early summer to early fall. It is drought-tolerant, thrives in full sun, and attracts a variety of pollinators.

Garden Tip

For a big garden, you can either fill the spaces with a variety of plants to create a lush, full look or incorporate stepping stones and pathways to add structure and visual interest.

Plants:

- Aster (1)
- Butterfly weed (9)
- Coreopsis (15)
- Daylily (17)
- Dogwood (18)
- Ninebark (34)
- Phlox (38)

Benchwarmers:

Goldenrod (26)
Hydrangea (28)
Lamb's ear (30)

I want plants for sandy soil.

Optimize your garden for sandy soil with a selection of plants that thrive in these conditions. These resilient plants will add color and texture to your garden, making the most of your unique soil type.

Butterfly Weed

Butterfly weed is a drought-tolerant perennial with striking orange flowers that bloom from early summer to fall. It's an excellent choice for sandy soils, providing bright color and attracting butterflies.

Cosmos

Cosmos are easy-to-grow annuals with delicate, daisy-like flowers that come in a variety of colors. They are well-suited for sandy soils and add a light, airy feel to your garden.

Joe Pye Weed

Joe Pye weed is a tall perennial with clusters of pinkish-purple flowers that bloom in late summer. It thrives in sandy soils and is known for attracting butterflies and other pollinators.

Russian Sage

Russian sage is a hardy perennial with tall spikes of lavender-blue flowers and aromatic silvery foliage. It thrives in sandy soils and adds a touch of elegance to your garden.

Native Plant Tip

The native plant Joe Pye weed is highly attractive to butterflies and bees, and its tall, sturdy stems can reach heights of more than 5 feet, providing an amazing vertical to your garden.

Garden Tip

Consider adding organic matter to sandy soil to improve moisture retention and fertility, but continue to choose plants that are well-adapted to these conditions for best results.

Plants:

- Butterfly weed (9)
- Cosmos (16)
- Joe Pye weed (29)
- Russian sage (41)

Benchwarmers:

Blanket flower (6)
Goldenrod (26)
Liatris (31)

I want plants for clay soil.

Clay soil, known for its dense and heavy texture, can pose a challenge for many plants due to its tendency to retain water and slow drainage. However, with the right plant choices, you can turn this challenge into an opportunity to create a beautiful garden.

Aster

Asters are hardy perennials with star-shaped flowers that bloom in late summer and fall. They add vibrant color to clay soils and attract pollinators.

Black-Eyed Susan

Black-eyed Susans are resilient perennials with bright yellow petals and dark centers. They bloom from summer to fall, thriving in clay soils and adding cheerful color to your garden.

Daylily

Daylilies are robust perennials known for their trumpet-shaped flowers in a variety of colors. They perform well in clay soils and provide continuous blooms from early summer to fall.

Feather Reed Grass

An ornamental grass with tall, slender stems and feathery plumes that add texture and movement to your garden, feather reed grass thrives in clay soils and is particularly low-maintenance.

Native Plant Tip

Many native grasses have deep root systems that help improve soil structure and drainage over time, a great help with heavy soil challenges.

Garden Tip

When working with clay soil, it's beneficial to incorporate organic matter such as compost to enhance soil structure and improve drainage.

Plants:

- Aster (1)
- Black-eyed Susan (5)
- Daylily (17)
- Feather reed grass (20)

Benchwarmers:

Bee balm (3)

Phlox (38)

Viburnum (49)

I want a drought-tolerant garden.

Design a garden that flourishes even in dry conditions with a selection of drought-tolerant plants. These resilient plants are not only water efficient but also provide vibrant colors and textures that will keep your garden looking great throughout the growing season. By choosing plants that thrive with minimal water, you can create a sustainable garden that reduces water usage.

Blanket Flower

Blanket flower is a hardy perennial that produces vibrant red and yellow blooms. It's highly drought-tolerant, thriving in full sun and well-drained soil and attracting butterflies and bees.

Coreopsis

This is a resilient perennial with bright yellow flowers that bloom throughout summer. It is drought-tolerant and perfect for adding cheerful color to your garden.

Feather Reed Grass

Feather reed grass is known for its tall, slender stems and feathery plumes. This ornamental grass thrives in dry conditions, adding texture and movement to your garden with minimal water required.

Goldenrod

Goldenrod is a drought-tolerant perennial that produces tall spikes of bright yellow flowers in late summer and fall. It attracts a variety of pollinators and adds a burst of color to your garden.

Russian Sage

Russian sage is a hardy perennial with tall spikes of lavender-blue flowers and aromatic silvery foliage. It thrives in dry conditions, providing long-lasting color and a touch of elegance to your garden.

Sedum

This succulent thrives in dry, rocky soils. Its fleshy leaves and clusters of star-shaped flowers add unique texture and color to your garden, and it requires very little water.

Native Plant Tip

Showy goldenrod (*Solidago speciosa*) is a native perennial that flourishes in dry soils and provides clusters of bright yellow flowers in late summer, making it a magnet for pollinators and a standout in drought-tolerant gardens.

Garden Tip

Mulch around your plants to help retain soil moisture and reduce evaporation. Consider using drip irrigation or soaker hoses to deliver water directly to the roots, minimizing water waste.

Plants:

- Blanket flower (6)
- Coreopsis (15)
- Feather reed grass (20)
- Goldenrod (26)
- Russian sage (41)
- Sedum (43)

Benchwarmers:

Black-eyed Susan (5)
Daylily (17)
Purple coneflower (39)

I want an animal-themed garden.

Turn your garden into a whimsical haven with plants that have animal-themed names. These selections will not only add beauty and variety to your garden, but also create a playful and engaging space for you and your visitors.

Bee Balm

This one produces vibrant, tubular flowers that are highly attractive to bees, butterflies, and hummingbirds. The flowers come in shades of red, pink, and purple, adding a splash of color and life to your garden.

Butterfly Weed

Known for its bright orange clusters of flowers that bloom from early summer to early fall, this plant is a magnet for butterflies, especially monarchs, and adds a lively touch to your garden.

Catmint

Catmint features soft, aromatic foliage and spikes of lavender-blue flowers that attract bees and butterflies. Its name comes from its appeal to cats, making it a fun and functional addition to your garden.

Lamb's Ear

Gardeners love this plant for its soft, velvety leaves that resemble a lamb's ear. This groundcover produces spikes of purple flowers in late spring to early summer, adding texture and charm to your garden.

Native Plant Tip

Butterfly weed is a native perennial that produces bright orange flowers, attracting butterflies and other pollinators. It thrives in well-drained soil and full sun, making it a perfect addition to your animal-themed garden.

Garden Tip

To enhance the playful animal theme, consider adding garden decor that complements the plant names, such as bee-shaped stakes near the bee balm or butterfly ornaments by the butterfly weed.

Plants:

- Bee balm (3)
- Butterfly weed (9)
- Catmint (12)
- Lamb's ear (30)

Benchwarmers:

Cardinal flower (11)

Dogwood (18)

Plant Directory

1 Aster

Symphyotrichum novae-angliae and cultivars

Plant type: Perennial
Hardiness: Zones 3–8
Size: Up to 6 ft. tall and 3 ft. wide
Flower color: Pink, purple, white, blue
Soil: Moist, rich
Light needs: Full sun to part shade
Attracts: Bees, butterflies, hummingbirds

Add a splash of color to your garden with these cheerful, daisy-like flowers. Blooming from summer to fall, asters have bright yellow centers and plenty of vibrant petals. They're reliable perennials, coming back every year. They're also called New England asters. To keep your asters thriving, divide them every few years in spring and share the extras with fellow gardeners.

2 Beautyberry

Callicarpa americana and cultivars

Plant type: Tree or shrub
Hardiness: Zones 6–10
Size: Up to 6 ft. tall and 6 ft. wide
Flower color: Small pink or purple flowers but most known for bright berries
Soil: Well-draining soil, can also tolerate clay
Light needs: Full sun to part shade
Attracts: Birds

Brighten up your garden with the vibrant purple or magenta berries of the beautyberry shrub. It's a magnet for birds in summer and fall, offering them a tasty treat. Easy to grow and disease-free, this shrub is an excellent addition to any wildlife-friendly garden. Prune beautyberry shrubs in late winter to early spring to encourage more vigorous growth and abundant berry production.

3 Bee Balm

Monarda didyma cultivars

Plant type: Perennial

Hardiness: Zones 4–9

Size: Up to 5 ft. tall and 3 ft. wide

Flower color: Red, pink, purple, lavender

Soil: Medium, well-drained

Light needs: Full sun to part shade

Attracts: Bees, birds, butterflies, hummingbirds

Bee balm is a must-have for any garden looking to attract bees, birds, and butterflies. This vibrant perennial is easy to grow and beloved by gardeners focused on native plants, with varieties suited for many regions. Divide bee balm plants every few years to prevent overcrowding and enhance air circulation, reducing the risk of powdery mildew.

4 Bellflower

Campanula americana

Plant type: Perennial, annual
Hardiness: Zones 4–7
Size: Up to 6 ft. tall and 2 ft. wide
Flower color: Blue and purple
Soil: Moist, well-drained
Light needs: Full sun to part shade
Attracts: Bees, butterflies, hummingbirds

Known for its stunning true blue blooms, bellflower is a top choice for attracting hummingbirds to your garden. Growing several feet tall, it bursts into color from mid- to late summer, and you can grow it as a perennial, annual, or even in containers. It's sometimes referred to as tall bellflower or American bellflower. Bellflowers are also known for their edible blossoms, which can be used to add a splash of color to salads and desserts.

5 Black-Eyed Susan

Rudbeckia fulgida and cultivars

Plant type: Perennial

Hardiness: Zones 3–9

Size: Up to 4 ft. tall and 3 ft. wide

Flower color: Golden yellow

Soil: Dry to medium well-drained soil

Light needs: Full sun to part shade

Attracts: Bees, birds, butterflies, hummingbirds

Brighten up your garden with the resilient black-eyed Susan, a perennial favorite known for its sunny yellow blooms. Tolerant of various soils and conditions, this hardy plant comes back stronger each year, providing a reliable food source for birds and attracting an array of wildlife. You may hear it called by its botanical name, rudbeckia. Gardeners often use black-eyed Susans for natural pest control because their bright flowers attract beneficial insects.

6 Blanket Flower

Gaillardia ×grandiflora

Plant type: Perennial
Hardiness: Zones 3–10
Size: Up to 2 ft. tall and 2 ft. wide
Flower color: Mixture of yellow, orange, and red
Soil: Medium, well-drained
Light needs: Full sun
Attracts: Bees, birds, butterflies, hummingbirds

Brighten your garden with the colors of blanket flower, a hardy perennial that thrives in sunny spots. These resilient blooms attract bees and other pollinators, making them a great addition to wildlife-friendly gardens. Once established, blanket flowers return year after year. It is drought-tolerant once established, making it an excellent choice for low-water gardens.

7 Bleeding Heart

Lamprocapnos spectabilis

Plant type: Perennial

Hardiness: Zones 3–9

Size: Up to 3 ft. tall and wide

Flower color: Pink, white

Soil: Average, well-drained

Light needs: Part to full shade

Attracts: Bees, butterflies, hummingbirds

Bring a touch of romance to your garden with the enchanting bleeding heart, known for its unique, heart-shaped flowers. This perennial is a shade lover and an early bloomer, providing much-needed nectar for hummingbirds returning from migration in the spring. Bleeding hearts go dormant in the heat of summer, so plant them alongside summer-blooming perennials to keep your garden colorful all season long.

8 Bluebells

Mertensia virginica

Plant type: Perennial

Hardiness: Zones 3–8

Size: Up to 2 ft. tall and wide

Flower color: Blue, purple

Soil: Moist, well-drained

Light needs: Part sun to full shade

Attracts: Bees, butterflies, hummingbirds

Bluebells bring a magical touch to any garden with their stunning transformation from pale pink buds to deep blue flowers. These low-maintenance perennials thrive in shady spots and improve with each passing year, offering a lush display with minimal effort. Bluebells are one of the first flowers to bloom in spring, providing early nectar for pollinators. They're sometimes called Virginia bluebells.

9 Butterfly Weed

Asclepias tuberosa

Plant type: Perennial

Hardiness: Zones 3–9

Size: Up to 3 ft. tall and 2 ft. wide

Flower color: Orange

Soil: Medium, well-drained

Light needs: Full sun

Attracts: Bees, butterflies, hummingbirds

Butterfly weed is a vibrant perennial that stands out with its bright orange blooms, attracting a host of butterflies and other pollinators. As a member of the milkweed family, it's an essential plant for monarch caterpillars and thrives in a variety of soil conditions, making it a great choice for any garden. Butterfly weed has deep taproots that help it survive drought conditions. This makes it an excellent choice for low-maintenance gardens.

10 Buttonbush

Cephalanthus occidentalis

Plant type: Tree or shrub
Hardiness: Zones 5–9
Size: Up to 12 ft. tall and 8 ft. wide
Flower color: White
Soil: Moist, humus-rich soil
Light needs: Full sun to part shade
Attracts: Bees, butterflies, hummingbirds

Buttonbush is a standout shrub with its unique, ball-shaped, spiky blooms that attract a variety of pollinators. This hardy plant thrives in moist environments and requires little care, making it a perfect choice for gardeners looking to support bees and other wildlife. Buttonbush can grow in standing water, making it an excellent choice for rain gardens or planting near ponds and wetlands.

11 Cardinal Flower

Lobelia cardinalis

Plant type: Perennial

Hardiness: Zones 3–9

Size: Up to 4 ft. tall and 2 ft. wide

Flower color: Red, white, pink

Soil: Rich, medium, wet

Light needs: Full sun to part shade

Attracts: Bees, butterflies, hummingbirds

Cardinal flower always stands out with its vivid red tubular blooms that are perfect for attracting hummingbirds. This moisture-loving perennial thrives in wet areas, making it an excellent choice for planting near water features or in consistently damp soil. Cardinal flowers can thrive in both full sun and part shade, making them versatile for various garden settings.

12 Catmint

Nepeta species and cultivars

Plant type: Perennial
Hardiness: Zones 3–8
Size: Up to 3 ft. tall and 4 ft. wide
Flower color: Blue, purple
Soil: Well-drained, humus-rich
Light needs: Full sun
Attracts: Bees, butterflies, hummingbirds

Catmint is a gardener's favorite for its resilience and continuous growth, even in challenging conditions. Its silvery-green foliage and long-lasting purple blooms provide a lovely contrast in the garden, while its minty fragrance adds a refreshing touch. Catmint is deer resistant, making it an excellent choice for gardens where deer are a common problem.

13 Columbine

Aquilegia canadensis

Plant type: Perennial

Hardiness: Zones 3–8

Size: Up to 3 ft. tall and 2 ft. wide

Flower color: Light pink and yellow or red and yellow

Soil: Medium, well-drained

Light needs: Full sun to part shade

Attracts: Bees, butterflies, hummingbirds

Columbine adds a delicate charm to any garden with its unique flowers and early bloom time, making it a favorite for attracting hummingbirds. Once established, this perennial reliably returns each year, providing an early nectar source when few other plants are in bloom. Columbine flowers are edible and can add a splash of color to salads or desserts.

14 Coral Bells

Heuchera species and cultivars

Plant type: Perennial

Hardiness: Zones 4–9

Size: Up to 3 ft. tall and 2 ft. wide

Flower color: Many colors, including red, pink, and white

Soil: Rich, well-drained

Light needs: Full sun to full shade

Attracts: Bees, butterflies, hummingbirds

This shade-tolerant perennial is known for its stunning foliage that comes in a wide range of colors from deep purple to bright green. With delicate blooms that rise on tall stems, this plant is a surprising favorite for attracting hummingbirds and other pollinators. You'll often hear it called by its botanical name, heuchera (pronounced "*hew*-ker-uh"). You will find so many different combinations for coral bells, both for foliage and bloom color. Research different varieties to find your favorite.

15 Coreopsis

Coreopsis lanceolata and cultivars

Plant type: Perennial

Hardiness: Zones 4–9

Size: Up to 3 ft. tall and 2 ft. wide

Flower color: Yellow, but newer varieties are red, white, and bicolor

Soil: Medium, well-drained

Light needs: Full sun

Attracts: Bees, birds, butterflies, hummingbirds

Coreopsis, with its bright and cheerful yellow blooms, is a resilient perennial perfect for tough soil and drought conditions. Blooming throughout the summer, it provides a reliable source of nectar for hummingbirds and butterflies, and its seeds are a favorite of birds. Coreopsis is highly adaptable and can thrive in poor soils, making it an excellent choice for low-maintenance gardens and difficult planting sites.

16 Cosmos

Cosmos bipinnatus

Plant type: Annual

Hardiness: Zones 2–11

Size: Up to 4 ft. tall and 3 ft. wide

Flower color: Red, pink, white, yellow

Soil: Average, well-drained

Light needs: Full sun

Attracts: Bees, birds, butterflies, hummingbirds

These low-maintenance annuals are incredibly easy to grow from seed, making them a great choice for beginner gardeners and kids. The flowers not only attract bees, butterflies, and hummingbirds with their nectar but also provide seeds for birds later in the season, often reseeding themselves for next year. Cosmos can tolerate poor soil conditions and still produce abundant blooms, making them an ideal choice for less fertile garden areas.

17 Daylily

Hemerocallis species and cultivars

Plant type: Perennial

Hardiness: Zones 3–9

Size: Up to 3 ft. tall and wide

Flower color: Nearly every color except blue

Soil: Medium, well-drained

Light needs: Full sun to part shade

Attracts: Bees, butterflies, hummingbirds

Daylilies have lush foliage and plenty of beautiful blooms throughout the season. Despite each flower lasting only a day, these hardy perennials continuously produce new blossoms, providing a reliable food source for butterflies, bees, and hummingbirds. Daylilies are exceptionally low-maintenance and drought-tolerant, making them perfect for busy gardeners and less-than-ideal garden conditions.

18 Dogwood

Cornus species and cultivars

Plant type: Tree or shrub
Hardiness: Zones 5–9
Size: Up to 30 feet tall and wide
Flower color: White, pink
Soil: Medium, well-drained
Light needs: Full sun to part shade
Attracts: Bees, birds, butterflies, hummingbirds

It's easy to find one, two, or even five different dogwoods to grow in your yard because there are many shrubs and trees to choose from. Dogwoods offer year-round appeal: beautiful spring blooms, lush summer foliage, and vibrant berries in fall and winter. Flowering dogwood (*Cornus florida*) is a classic choice, but many other varieties can suit your garden needs—just ask your local garden center for recommendations. Red-twig dogwood (*Cornus sericea*) is another excellent choice for attracting wildlife, offering striking red stems that add winter interest to your garden.

19 Elderberry

Sambucus canadensis

Plant type: Tree or shrub

Hardiness: Zones 3–9

Size: Up to 12 ft. tall and wide

Flower color: White

Soil: Medium, well-drained

Light needs: Full sun to part shade

Attracts: Bees, birds, butterflies, hummingbirds

Elderberry is a fantastic addition to any garden, especially in colder regions. In spring, these shrubs produce clusters of tiny white flowers with a delightful lemony scent, which transform into dark, rich berries by late summer. Not only are these berries great for making jams, jellies, and wines, but they also provide a valuable food source for birds. Elderberries are known for their medicinal properties and often used in traditional remedies to boost the immune system and fight off colds and flu.

20 Feather Reed Grass

Calamagrostis ×acutiflora

Plant type: Perennial
Hardiness: Zones 5–9
Size: Up to 5 ft. tall and 3 ft. wide
Flower color: Not significant but pinkish purple
Soil: Medium to wet soil
Light needs: Full sun
Attracts: Birds

Feather reed grass is a must-have for wildlife-friendly gardens, known for its striking vertical presence and the popular cultivar 'Karl Foerster'. This ornamental grass produces wheat-like seed heads in late spring, providing a valuable food source for birds and lasting through fall. Feather reed grass is incredibly versatile, thriving in a variety of conditions including part shade, clay soil, and even drought.

21 Floss Flower

Ageratum houstonianum

Plant type: Annual

Hardiness: Zones 2–11

Size: Up to 3 ft. tall and 2 ft. wide

Flower color: Purple, blue

Soil: Moist, well-drained

Light needs: Full sun to part shade

Attracts: Bees, butterflies, hummingbirds

Floss flowers, with their fuzzy blooms and vibrant purple and blue hues, add a unique charm to any garden. These annuals are a butterfly magnet and can be easily grown from seed or found as starter plants at garden centers. You may hear them referred to as ageratum, which is also their botanical name. Floss flowers make excellent container plants, adding a pop of color and attracting pollinators to patios and balconies.

22 Fountain Grass

Pennisetum alopecuroides and cultivars

Plant type: Perennial
Hardiness: Zones 6–9
Size: Up to 5 ft. tall and wide
Flower color: Silver to pinkish white
Soil: Medium to wet soil
Light needs: Full sun to part shade
Attracts: Birds

Fountain grass is a versatile and low-maintenance ornamental grass that provides food and shelter for birds year-round. Ideal for perennial beds, borders, or as a standalone feature, it adds rich golden hues in fall that transition to beige in the winter. Fountain grass is deer resistant, making it an excellent choice for gardens in areas where deer are common.

23 Four O'Clocks

Mirabilis jalapa

Plant type: Annual or tender perennial
Hardiness: Zones 9–11
Size: Up to 3 ft. tall and wide
Flower color: Pink, red, magenta, yellow, white
Soil: Wide range of soils, well-draining
Light needs: Full sun to partial shade
Attracts: Bees, butterflies, hummingbirds

Four o'clocks, native to Peru, are known for their vibrant, exotic-looking flowers that attract hummingbirds and other pollinators. These versatile plants are perfect for containers, patios, or hanging baskets, and they bloom throughout summer, adding a splash of color to any garden space. Four o'clocks open their fragrant flowers in late afternoon and evening, providing a delightful scent and attracting nighttime pollinators like moths.

24 Fuchsia

Fuchsia cultivars

Plant type: Annual or tender perennial
Hardiness: Zone 10–11
Size: Up to 2 ft. tall and wide
Flower color: Red, pink, white, violet, purple, bicolor
Soil: Medium, well-drained
Light needs: Part shade to full shade
Attracts: Bees, butterflies, hummingbirds

Fuchsia is a favorite for shady gardens, known for its striking, dancer-like flowers in vibrant shades of pink, purple, and red. Often seen in hanging baskets, these plants provide a stunning display from spring through early fall, attracting bees, butterflies, and hummingbirds. Fuchsia is ideal for adding color to shaded areas of your garden and can be successfully overwintered indoors.

25 Geranium

Pelargonium cultivars

Plant type: Annual or tender perennial
Hardiness: Zones 10–11
Size: Up to 3 ft. tall and wide
Flower color: Red, orange, pink, purple, white, bicolor
Soil: Wide range, well-draining
Light needs: Full sun to part shade
Attracts: Bees, butterflies, hummingbirds

Geraniums are reliable and versatile plants that thrive in challenging spots, whether in your garden or on your patio. Known for their vibrant blooms that last from spring to fall, these hardy annuals tolerate a wide range of conditions and attract hummingbirds, adding life and color to any space. Geraniums can be easily propagated from cuttings, allowing you to expand your garden or share plants with friends effortlessly.

26 Goldenrod

Solidago speciosa

Plant type: Perennial
Hardiness: Zones 3–8
Size: Up to 3 ft. tall and wide
Flower color: Yellow
Soil: Average, well-drained
Light needs: Full sun
Attracts: Bees, birds, butterflies, hummingbirds

Goldenrod is a hardy and reliable perennial known for its bright yellow blooms that bring a splash of color from summer to late fall. Thriving in a variety of conditions, this native wildflower is drought-resistant and offers consistent nectar and seed sources for a variety of wildlife, making it a great choice for challenging garden spots. Goldenrod is an important late-season food source for pollinators, providing essential nectar and pollen when many other flowers have finished blooming.

27 Hosta

Hosta cultivars

Plant type: Perennial

Hardiness: Zones 3–8

Size: Up to 4 ft. tall and 6 ft. wide

Flower color: Purple, white

Soil: Average, well-draining

Light needs: Sun to shade

Attracts: Bees, butterflies, hummingbirds

Hostas are well-loved for their lush, attractive foliage and their ability to thrive in shaded areas. What many gardeners don't realize is that their delicate flowers, which emerge from tall stalks, are a rich source of nectar, making them an excellent choice for attracting hummingbirds even in the darkest corners of your garden. Hostas can vary greatly in size and color, offering hundreds of varieties to suit any garden design, from small border plants to large, dramatic focal points.

28 Hydrangea

Hydrangea species and cultivars

Plant type: Tree or shrub
Hardiness: Zones 5–9
Size: Up to 6 ft. tall and 10 ft. wide
Flower color: Blue, pink, purple, red, white
Soil: Acidic, well-drained
Light needs: Full sun to part shade
Attracts: Bees, birds, butterflies, hummingbirds

Hydrangeas are garden favorites known for their stunning and abundant blooms. While they can be a bit tricky to establish, once they take root, these shrubs are reliable and will grace your garden with beautiful globe-shaped or flattened flower heads for many years, attracting bees, butterflies, and hummingbirds. Note the flower color of bigleaf hydrangea (*Hydrangea macrophylla*) and its cultivars can change based on soil pH—acidic soils produce blue flowers, while alkaline soils yield pink blooms.

29 Joe Pye Weed

Eutrochium purpureum

Plant type: Perennial

Hardiness: Zones 4–9

Size: Up to 7 ft. tall and 4 ft. wide

Flower color: Pinkish red

Soil: Moist, rich

Light needs: Full sun to part shade

Attracts: Bees, birds, butterflies, hummingbirds

Joe Pye weed is a resilient native perennial that thrives in wet, challenging environments like swamps and riverbanks. With its tall stature and clusters of pinkish-red blooms, it serves as an important nectar and seed source for a variety of wildlife, making it an excellent addition to any native garden. In fact, Joe Pye weed is a magnet for monarch butterflies, providing a crucial nectar source during their migration period.

30 Lamb's Ear

Stachys byzantina

Plant type: Perennial

Hardiness: Zones 4–8

Size: Up to 1 ft. tall and wide

Flower color: Purple, pink

Soil: Medium, well-drained

Light needs: Full sun to part shade

Attracts: Bees, butterflies

Lamb's ear is a perennial favorite for its soft, silvery green foliage that adds unique texture to any garden. This plant not only provides visual interest but also attracts bees and butterflies with its subtle purple or pink blooms. Lamb's ear leaves are often used in children's gardens due to their soft, fuzzy texture, which can be a tactile delight for young gardeners.

31 Liatris

Liatris spicata

Plant type: Perennial
Hardiness: Zones 3–8
Size: Up to 4 ft. tall and 2 ft. wide
Flower color: Purple
Soil: Average, well-drained
Light needs: Full sun
Attracts: Bees, butterflies, hummingbirds

Liatris, with its tall, spiky blooms, adds a dramatic vertical element to any garden. Known for its fuzzy, purple flowers, this perennial is a magnet for hummingbirds, butterflies, and bees, making it a vibrant and lively addition during its bloom time. It's sometimes referred to as blazing star or gayfeather. Liatris blooms from the top down, which is unusual for flowering plants, and adds an interesting visual effect as the flowers gradually open along the spike.

32 Lungwort

Pulmonaria species and cultivars

Plant type: Perennial

Hardiness: Zones 3–8

Size: Up to 1 ft. tall and 2 ft. wide

Flower color: Blue, purple, pink, white

Soil: Moist, well-draining

Light needs: Part sun to full shade

Attracts: Bees, butterflies, hummingbirds

Lungwort is a shade-loving perennial prized for its attractive spotted or variegated foliage that often remains vibrant into fall and winter. Its small, colorful flowers, which come in shades of blue, purple, pink, and white, are excellent for attracting hummingbirds and other pollinators to your garden. Lungwort is one of the first perennials to bloom in early spring, providing an important early nectar source for pollinators.

33 Milkweed

Asclepias syriaca

Plant type: Perennial

Hardiness: Zones 3–9

Size: Up to 5 ft. tall and 1 ft. wide

Flower color: Pink, white

Soil: Medium, well-drained

Light needs: Full sun

Attracts: Bees, butterflies

Milkweed is an essential perennial for anyone looking to support the monarch butterfly population. This plant serves as the sole host for monarch eggs and caterpillars, while its nectar-rich blooms attract a wide variety of butterflies and bees, making it a vital addition to pollinator gardens. Milkweed produces a milky sap containing compounds that make monarch caterpillars and butterflies toxic to predators, providing them with a crucial defense mechanism.

34 Ninebark

Physocarpus opulifolius and cultivars

Plant type: Tree or shrub

Hardiness: Zones 2–8

Size: Up to 8 ft. tall and 6 ft. wide

Flower color: White or pink

Soil: Medium, well-drained, slightly acidic

Light needs: Full sun to part shade

Attracts: Bees, birds, butterflies, hummingbirds

Ninebark is a hardy and versatile shrub known for its beautiful, nectar-rich blooms in spring and its attractive fruit in late summer and fall. This resilient plant thrives in a wide range of climates and provides year-round interest with its peeling, multicolored bark. Ninebark's dense foliage and structure make it an excellent choice for creating natural privacy screens and windbreaks in your garden.

35 Pansy

Viola ×wittrockiana

Plant type: Annual or tender perennial
Hardiness: Zones 7–10
Size: Up to 10 in. tall and 1 ft. wide
Flower color: Red, orange, yellow, blue, violet, white, pink, bicolor
Soil: Medium, well-drained
Light needs: Full sun to part shade
Attracts: Bees, butterflies

Pansies are beloved by gardeners for their vibrant colors and early spring blooms, making them a go-to choice for brightening up beds and containers. These hardy flowers provide essential nectar and pollen for early-emerging bees and butterflies, and they continue to bloom for several months, offering lasting beauty and support for pollinators. Pansies are not only popular in spring but also make excellent fall plantings, providing much-needed resources for late-season bees and butterflies.

36 Penstemon

Penstemon species and cultivars

Plant type: Perennial
Hardiness: Zones 3–10
Size: Up to 4 ft. wide and 2 ft. tall
Flower color: Red, pink, purple, blue, white
Soil: Well-draining, sandy
Light needs: Part shade to full sun
Attracts: Bees, butterflies, hummingbirds

Penstemon, with its striking tubular flowers in vibrant shades, is a magnet for hummingbirds and other pollinators. Once it settles in, this hardy perennial reliably returns each year, providing continuous blooms throughout the summer. Penstemon is drought-tolerant once established, making it a great option for xeriscaping and low-water gardens.

37 Petunia

Petunia cultivars

Plant type: Annual or tender perennial
Hardiness: Zones 10–11
Size: Up to 2 ft. tall and 3 ft. wide
Flower color: Available in most colors, including bicolor
Soil: Medium, well-draining
Light needs: Part shade to full sun
Attracts: Bees, butterflies, hummingbirds

Petunias are a favorite annual for containers and hanging baskets due to their ease of growth, long blooming period, and attractiveness to hummingbirds, bees, and butterflies. These versatile flowers come in a range of colors, allowing gardeners to create stunning displays that thrive even in less-than-ideal soil and water conditions. Petunias are known for their resilience and can bounce back quickly after heavy rain, making them a reliable choice for consistent garden color.

38 Phlox

Phlox paniculata cultivars

Plant type: Perennial

Hardiness: Zones 4–8

Size: Up to 4 ft. tall and 3 ft. wide

Flower color: Pink, purple, red, coral, white, bicolor

Soil: Medium-well-drained

Light needs: Full sun to part shade

Attracts: Bees, butterflies, hummingbirds

Phlox, or garden phlox, is known for its long blooming period and vibrant clusters of flowers. Easy to establish and maintain, it reliably returns each year, providing up to three months of color and attracting a variety of pollinators, including bees and butterflies. Regularly deadheading phlox by removing old blooms encourages continuous flowering, keeping your garden vibrant and colorful throughout the growing season.

39 Purple Coneflower

Echinacea purpurea and cultivars

Plant type: Perennial

Hardiness: Zones 4–9

Size: Up to 4 ft. tall and 2 ft. wide

Flower color: Pink

Soil: Medium, well-drained

Light needs: Full sun to part shade

Attracts: Bees, birds, butterflies, hummingbirds

Purple coneflower is a must-have perennial for any garden, known for its striking pink blooms and resilience. These hardy plants are drought-tolerant, easy to grow, and attract a variety of wildlife, including bees, butterflies, hummingbirds, and birds. Over time, a single plant can multiply, enhancing your garden's beauty and ecological value. Leave the flower heads on the plant to provide a natural food source for birds, especially finches, during the winter months.

40 Rose of Sharon

Hibiscus syriacus and cultivars

Plant type: Tree or shrub
Hardiness: Zones 5–8
Size: Up to 12 ft. tall and 10 ft. wide
Flower color: Pink, purple, blue, white, bicolor
Soil: Medium, well-draining
Light needs: Part shade to full sun
Attracts: Bees, butterflies, hummingbirds

Rose of Sharon, with its tropical-looking flowers, is a versatile and hardy shrub or tree that's closely related to hibiscus. This easy-to-establish plant boasts a long bloom time, making it an excellent choice for attracting hummingbirds, butterflies, and bees throughout the season. Rose of Sharon can be pruned in late winter or early spring to maintain its shape and encourage more prolific blooming next season.

41 Russian Sage

Perovskia atriplicifolia

Plant type: Perennial

Hardiness: Zones 4–9

Size: Up to 5 ft. tall and 4 ft. wide

Flower color: Purple, lavender, blue

Soil: Medium, well-drained

Light needs: Full sun

Attracts: Bees, butterflies, hummingbirds

Russian sage is a striking perennial that captivates gardeners with its tall, wispy spikes of lavender-blue flowers. This hardy plant is drought-tolerant, low maintenance, and thrives in a variety of soils, making it a versatile addition to any garden. Russian sage's aromatic foliage can repel certain pests, making it a great companion plant in vegetable and flower gardens.

42 Salvia

Salvia species and cultivars

Plant type: Annual or tender perennial
Hardiness: Zones 8–10
Size: Up to 3 ft. tall and wide
Flower color: Blue, purple, red
Soil: Medium, well-draining
Light needs: Part shade to full sun
Attracts: Bees, butterflies, hummingbirds

Salvia is a diverse and vibrant group, offering many popular plants like aromatic pineapple sage (*Salvia elegans*) and striking red-blooming *Salvia greggii*. These are excellent nectar sources, making them perfect for attracting hummingbirds and other pollinators. Plant them in sunny spots and water regularly to enjoy blooms through early fall. Salvia is known for its long blooming season, often providing vibrant color and nectar from late spring through early fall.

43 Sedum

Sedum cultivars

Plant type: Perennial

Hardiness: Zones 4–9

Size: Up to 3 ft. tall and wide

Flower color: Pink, red, white, yellow

Soil: Medium, well-drained, slightly alkaline

Light needs: Full sun

Attracts: Bees, butterflies

Sedum, also known as stonecrop, is a versatile and low-maintenance perennial ideal for gardens needing drought-tolerant plants. With its thick, succulent leaves and stems, sedum produces clusters of star-shaped blooms that create a striking display. Blooming from late summer through fall, it provides essential nectar for honeybees and butterflies during this critical period. Sedum is excellent for rock gardens and borders because its shallow roots help prevent soil erosion and its foliage adds texture and year-round interest.

44 Shasta Daisy

Leucanthemum ×superbum

Plant type: Perennial

Hardiness: Zones 5–9

Size: Up to 4 ft. tall and 3 ft. wide

Flower color: White

Soil: Dry to medium, well-drained

Light needs: Full sun

Attracts: Bees, birds, butterflies, hummingbirds

Shasta daisy is a versatile and charming perennial that thrives in a variety of garden settings, from borders and edges to containers and hummingbird gardens. Known for its classic white petals and yellow centers, this long-blooming flower provides nectar for pollinators and seeds for birds, making it a valuable addition to any wildlife-friendly garden. Shasta daisies can tolerate poor soil conditions, making them a hardy and low maintenance option for gardens with less-than-ideal soil.

45 Spirea

Spiraea species and culitvars

Plant type: Tree or shrub

Hardiness: Zones 3–8

Size: Up to 10 ft. tall and 8 ft. wide

Flower color: Pink, red, white, yellow

Soil: Medium, well-drained

Light needs: Full sun to part shade

Attracts: Bees, birds, butterflies, hummingbirds

Spirea is a versatile and hardy shrub that graces many backyards and public gardens with its beautiful blooms. Available in a wide range of types and sizes, spirea can be chosen to fit any garden space. Depending on the variety, these shrubs can offer colorful flowers from early summer through fall. Spirea is incredibly resilient and can tolerate a wide range of soil conditions, making it an excellent choice for low-maintenance gardens.

46 Summersweet

Clethra alnifolia

Plant type: Tree or shrub

Hardiness: Zones 3–9

Size: Up to 8 ft. tall and 6 ft. wide

Flower color: White, pink

Soil: Well-drained, slightly acidic

Light needs: Full sun to full shade

Attracts: Bees, birds, butterflies, hummingbirds

Summersweet, also known as sweet pepperbush, is an excellent choice for shady gardens, thriving in part to full shade with the right conditions. This hardy shrub produces fragrant, robust blooms in late summer, and its foliage transforms into a vibrant yellow in fall, adding seasonal interest to your garden. Summersweet's flowers are highly fragrant, attracting pollinators from afar and filling your garden with a sweet scent during its blooming period.

47 Sunflower

Helianthus annuus

Plant type: Annual

Hardiness: Zones 2–11

Size: Up to 10 ft. tall and 3 ft. wide

Flower color: Yellow, red, and bicolor

Soil: Average, well-drained

Light needs: Full sun

Attracts: Bees, birds, butterflies, hummingbirds

Sunflowers are vibrant and iconic additions to any garden, known for their tall, striking blooms and seed production. Easy to grow from seed, these annuals provide food for birds from summer through fall. With a variety of sizes and colors, including towering Mammoth types and more compact varieties, sunflowers can enhance any garden space. They can also be used as natural trellises for climbing plants like beans or morning glories, creating a beautiful and functional garden feature.

48 Veronica

Veronica cultivars

Plant type: Perennial
Hardiness: Zones 4–9
Size: Up to 2 ft. tall and wide
Flower color: Purple, blue, pink, white
Soil: Medium, well-drained
Light needs: Full sun
Attracts: Bees, butterflies, hummingbirds

Veronica, known for its tall, spiky blooms, adds a striking vertical element to any garden. This perennial is particularly popular with bees and butterflies thanks to its vibrant colors, including purple and true blue. For a standout blue bloom, consider cultivars like 'Crater Lake Blue' and 'Sunny Border Blue'. Regular deadheading of veronica flowers can encourage continuous blooming throughout the summer.

49 Viburnum

Viburnum species and cultivars

Plant type: Tree or shrub

Hardiness: Zones 3–9

Size: Up to 15 ft. tall and 12 ft. wide

Flower color: White

Soil: Medium, well-drained

Light needs: Full sun to part shade

Attracts: Bees, birds, butterflies, hummingbirds

Viburnum provides year-round interest and wildlife benefits. In spring, it offers beautiful white flowers that attract hummingbirds, butterflies, and bees. As the season progresses, it produces berries that persist into winter, providing a valuable food source for birds. Viburnum leaves often turn beautiful shades of red, orange, or purple in fall, providing stunning autumn foliage and adding seasonal interest to your garden.

50 Zinnia

Zinnia elegans

Plant type: Annual
Hardiness: Zones 2–11
Size: Up to 4 ft. tall and 1 ft. wide
Flower color: Orange, pink, purple, red, white, yellow, green, multicolor
Soil: Medium, well-draining
Light needs: Full sun
Attracts: Bees, butterflies, hummingbirds

Zinnias are vibrant and easy-to-grow annuals that add a burst of color to any garden. These hardy flowers bloom constantly from summer to fall, attracting hummingbirds, butterflies, and bees. Simply provide them with full sun and regular watering, and zinnias will reward you with a stunning display. To save zinnia seeds for the next season, allow the seedheads to dry completely on the plant. Once dry, gently shake out the seeds and store them for planting next year.

Frequently Asked Questions

Frequently Asked Questions

About the Plants

Why are there 50 plants featured?

The 50 plants featured in this book are some of the most common, resilient, and easy-to-grow options available to gardeners. These are tried-and-true recommendations that thrive in a wide range of environments across North America. I've chosen these plants because they have consistently proven themselves in gardens, making them reliable choices for anyone looking to create a beautiful and low-maintenance garden.

Can I mix and match from the 50 plants in the plant directory?

Absolutely! You're encouraged to mix and match the plants from the directory to suit your garden's needs. However, it's important to keep an eye on factors like soil conditions, light requirements, and space needs to ensure that the plants you choose will thrive together. Experimenting with different combinations can lead to some wonderfully unique garden designs.

Can I substitute plants that aren't in the plant directory?

Yes, you can substitute plants that aren't listed in the directory, especially if you're knowledgeable about plants or feel confident in selecting alternatives. Just be mindful of the same

considerations—light, soil, and size requirements—to ensure that your substitutions will work well within the plan.

How can I incorporate more native plants?

Incorporating more native plants into your garden is a wonderful way to support local ecosystems. Throughout this book, you'll find tips on choosing native plants that are well-suited to your region. Additionally, connecting with local plant organizations, native plant societies, or master gardener groups can provide you with valuable information and access to native plant options specific to your area.

Where do I find native plants?

To find native plants, seek out local sources such as native plant sales, specialty nurseries, and local garden centers that focus on regional flora. Native plants are often harder to find at big-box stores, so going local can really pay off. Local experts will also be able to provide advice tailored to your specific gardening environment.

About Your Garden

What if I don't know my garden's light needs?

Understanding your garden's light needs is crucial for plant success. The simplest way to determine this is by observing your garden on a sunny day. Track how many hours of sunlight each area receives. Full sun is typically defined as six or more hours of direct sunlight per day, partial sun or shade as two to six hours, and full shade as less than two hours. This information will guide you in choosing the right plants for each area.

What if I don't know my soil type?

If you're unsure about your soil type, consider doing a basic soil test. You can purchase a soil testing kit online or at a garden center, or you can perform simple DIY tests to determine if your

soil is sandy, clay, or loamy. Understanding your soil's composition will help you make better plant choices and amendments if necessary.

What if I have poor soil?

If a soil test reveals that your soil is less than ideal, don't worry—there are ways to improve it. Adding organic matter, such as compost, leaf mold, or well-rotted manure can greatly enhance soil structure and fertility. Incorporating these materials into your soil will help create a healthier environment for your plants to thrive.

What if I don't have enough room for the plants?

If you find that a planting plan includes more plants than your space can accommodate, it's easy to modify the plan. You can reduce the number of plants or eliminate a particular type if needed. The key is to adapt the plan so it fits your space while still creating a cohesive and attractive garden.

What if the plans aren't big enough for my large space?

On the other hand, if a planting plan seems too small for your large garden space, you can easily expand it. Add more plants to fill in the gaps or repeat the planting patterns to create a larger, more impactful garden. Adjusting the plan to suit your space is a great way to make the garden truly your own.

About Planting by Numbers

How long will it take to see results?

The timeline for seeing results depends on the types of plants used in the plan. For gardens that include annuals, you'll likely see blooms and growth within the first year. For perennials, it may take a year or two for the plants to become fully established. During this period, perennials may focus more on root development and less on flowering, so patience is key. With time, your garden will grow and reach its full potential.

Why am I not seeing bees, butterflies, or birds?

Most of the plants in these planting plans are designed to attract bees, butterflies, and birds, but it can take some time before you start to see these visitors regularly. They might be most active in your garden early in the morning or late in the evening, so you might miss them if you're not observing at those times. Additionally, avoiding the use of pesticides and sticking to the planting plan will help create a welcoming environment for these pollinators and wildlife.

Should I use seeds or plants?

Both seeds and plants have their advantages. If you're looking to save money and enjoy the process of growing plants from scratch, starting with seeds can be a rewarding option. This is particularly true for annuals, which can be started indoors in late winter or early spring. However, if you're aiming for quicker results or prefer a simpler approach, purchasing established plants is the way to go.

Where should I buy my plants?

Choosing where to buy your plants is a personal decision with many options available, especially online. However, I strongly recommend exploring local and native plant sources as much as possible. Local nurseries and garden centers often have staff with extensive knowledge of what works best in your area, and they can offer personalized advice that you won't get from big-box stores or online retailers. If you're unsure where to start, ask local gardeners for recommendations—they'll often know the best places to find quality plants.

About Maintaining Your Garden

Do I need to fertilize my garden?

Most gardens can benefit from occasional fertilization, but it can be intimidating to figure out what to use. Rather than focusing on synthetic fertilizers, consider adding organic matter to your soil. Compost, well-rotted manure, and other organic materials can naturally improve soil

fertility and structure, leading to healthier plants without the need for chemical fertilizers. If you're looking for guidance, check with a local expert or your area master gardener group.

Should I clean out my garden in fall?

Instead of doing a full garden clean-up in fall, consider leaving some plants standing through winter. Many gardeners cut their plants down to the ground in fall, but leaving them up can provide food and shelter for wildlife during the colder months. Additionally, leaving the plants in place can add visual interest to your garden in winter.

What if my plants get eaten early on?

If you're dealing with pests like rabbits or deer that nibble on your plants, it's important to protect young plants early on. Consider using physical barriers, like fencing or netting, to keep animals away until your plants are well established. Once the plants are stronger, they'll be better able to withstand occasional nibbling.

What if my plants get a disease?

If you notice signs of disease, such as discoloration or unusual spots on your plants, it's important to act quickly. Take photos of the affected plants and consult with your local garden center or a master gardener group to get a proper diagnosis. Early intervention can help prevent the disease from spreading and ensure your plants recover more quickly.

What if my plants get out of control?

It's common for plants to grow larger than expected, especially if they're thriving in their environment. If your garden starts to feel overgrown or unruly, take the time to assess whether your plants need to be pruned, divided, or moved. Overplanting can lead to crowding, so don't hesitate to thin out plants as needed. Splitting plants in the spring or fall can help manage their size and keep your garden looking neat. When in doubt, take photos and consult with an expert for advice.

What if weeds overtake my garden?

Weeds can quickly become a problem if not managed early on. The best approach is to stay vigilant and address weeds as soon as they appear. Regular weeding, combined with organic treatments like mulch and compost, can help suppress weed growth naturally. Mulch is particularly effective at blocking sunlight from reaching weed seeds, preventing them from germinating and spreading.

Photo and Illustration Credits

Dreamstime

Anthony Baggett, 155
Apugach5, 151, 157
Barmalini, 139
© Bluehand, 12
Candy1812, 172
Colin Mackenzie, 52
Countrymama, 170
Darko Plohl, 148
© Dawnmercer, 118
Diana Coman, 140
© Gerald D. Tang, 136, 143, 163
Gratysanna, 144
Hiroshi Tanaka, 167
Ihar Mamchyts, 149
© Iperl, 14
Iryna Rasko, 166
Iva Villi, 153
Jack Dean, 32
© John Anderson, 124
Jonny Mccullagh, 60
Justlight, 173
© Katyamaximenko, 132
Kazakovmaksim, 160
© Larry Metayer, 125, 126
© Larysa Ros, 137
LauraTabor, 64
Ieva Zemite, 141
Lianem, 159
Loflo69, 158
© Macsstock, 127
Mariia Boiko, 163
© Mashiki, 131, 171 (bottom)
© Matthew Omojola, 17
Maya Afzaal, 142
© Meunierd, 130
mzurawski, 24
Nikolay Stoimenov, 161
Olena Marina, 156
© Onepony, 7, 16
© Oseland, 120
Pakhnyushchyy, 171 (top)
© Pasqueflower, 134
Patrick Jennings, 28
Paul Lemke, 174
Paul Roedding, 128
Penpakn, 154
© Peter Mooy, 123
© Picturethisimages, 135
Prasit Rodphan, 145
© Prostockstudio, 9 (top)
Rita Puteikyte, 150
© Robert Buchel, 121
Robert Pearson, 175
© Roman Milert, 122
Sagegardenherbs, 147
Sarah_Robson, 152
Scattoselvaggio, 164
© Seaonwebaonweb, 10
Sgv230, 162
© Snehitdesign, 13
Steve Callahan, 146
© Svetakinzerskaya, 137
Svetlana Zhukova, 138
© Thamtaknot, 133
© Tracy Immordino, 119, 129

iStock

Aleksandr Krotkov, 68
Alex Manders, 104
Alfe, 80
Angelafoto, 84
Angelique Nijssen, 108
AwakenedEye, 72
bgwalker, 100, 112
david010167, 168
db_beyer, 20
Diane Labombarbe, 9 (bottom)
dreaming2004, 44
JudiParkinson, 76
Juhla, 18
manpuku7, 56
Nachcha Muangsan, 178
Nukopic, 180
ohishiistk, 176
ooyoo, 116
Oversnap, 15
patty_c, 40
RiverNorthPhotography, 88
Skhoward, 92
undefined undefined, 48
Whiteway, 37
ZICC, 96

Cover photos: Larry Metayer, Svetlana Zhukova, Sagegarden-herbs, Sgv230\Dreamstime; Jeffengeloutdoors.com\iStock

Garden illustrations by Brenda Lyons

Index

Photo: Tina Gregory

Stacy Tornio is the author of more than twenty books, including *The Ultimate Wildlife Habitat Garden* and *The National Parks Scavenger Hunt*. She loves writing about gardening and has shared her passion with readers on sites like Treehugger and HGTV. Stacy spent many years working on *Birds & Blooms* magazine, where she enjoyed exploring new flowers and finding native plants to add to her own yard. Her love for nature extends to her family, too—she co-wrote *101 Outdoor Adventures to Have Before You Grow Up* with her son, which won the National Outdoor Book Award. She also created the board game *Lucky Bears* with her daughter. Learn more about their adventures at Be a Good Human (beagoodhuman.co).